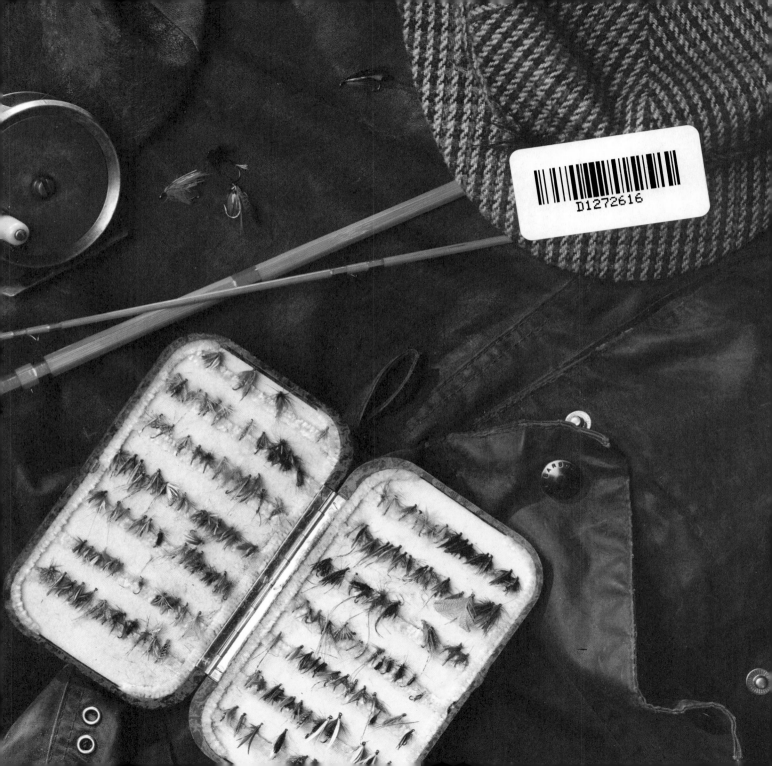

TROUT
Fly Fishing

RIZZOLI
NEW YORK

Philip White

First published in the United States of America in 1995
by RIZZOLI INTERNATIONAL PUBLICATIONS INC.
300 Park Avenue South, New York, NY 10010

Publisher:	Robin Burgess
Design & Publishing Manager:	Rachel Rush
Cover Photography:	Chris Allen, Forum Advertising Limited
Editor:	John Wilshaw
Illustrator(s):	Linden Artists
Photography:	Chris Allen, Forum Advertising Limited
Typesetting:	Seller's, Grantham
Colour separation:	GA Graphics, Stamford
Produced:	Imago, Singapore
Title:	TROUT Fly Tying
ISBN:	0-8478-1868-3
LC:	94-41900

Some of the flies described in this book originated in excess of a hundred years ago. They have withstood the test of time, technology, and "anglers myth" to remain as effective today as they have ever been.

For authenticity, the fly tying materials used are to the original and traditional recipes. These naturally occurring materials were originally chosen for their known behaviour and colouration when emersed in the water, and proven effectiveness over many years of subsequent use.

In certain countries, alternative or synthetic materials may be substituted if the original materials are not available.

Contents

Preface

Some say that the ability to fish is a sure sign of a badly spent youth. True or not, I was never out of water as a boy, cold when playing in it and very often a good deal warmer when I got home soaking!

I knew the whereabouts of every frog pond for miles and spent more than a few days constructing dams across streams at least two feet wide and six inches deep. Sadly these days, youngsters with a wanderlust cannot be let out of sight, never mind miles away from home, but that's progress.

By 12 years of age I was rarely without a rod, cycling the three miles to the river. Then I discovered fly fishing.

When my brother was not watching, I pinched his rod and was soon off in search of dace and grayling. Seeing my enthusiasm, an old chap gave me a couple of old greenheart salmon rods and some fishing books.

I cobbled those old salmon rods into trout rods and then wore my thumb out reading

Above: Fly reel from the 1850's.

Right: Turn of the century landing net.

those books. I drank in every word.

One had a chapter about fly dressing and my life was ruined. I became a compulsive fly dresser overnight. Feathers were plucked out of pillows and I haunted poulterers shops for game bird feathers.

I dressed those first flies in my fingers, but then birds of a very different feather took my fancy and all was forgotten for a few years. Happily, commonsense prevailed and I was soon back to a far more

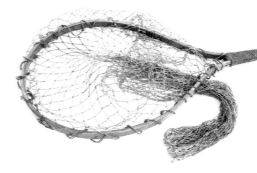

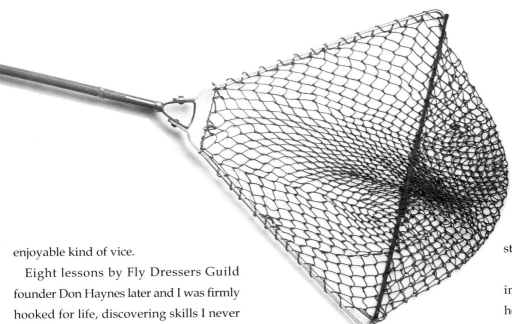

enjoyable kind of vice.

Eight lessons by Fly Dressers Guild founder Don Haynes later and I was firmly hooked for life, discovering skills I never thought I even possessed.

My future wife Mary, an accomplished fisher and shot, was one of my own early pupils and not many can say that their courting days, well quite a few of them, were spent fishing in two different boats!

My mind-numbing office job left behind, I landed a river keeper's job on the River Avon, in the south-east of England, at the ripe old age of 31.

I was assured that because I knew absolutely nothing about the job, I would quickly adapt to the way the owner wanted his river run. In those days, the river was one of the very first fully managed and

Above: An early flick-up landing net.

Below: Ivory handled Army and Navy reel.

stocked trout fisheries.

After an interlude at a private club water in Sussex, I moved to my present job as head river keeper to the Duke of Rutland on his Haddon Hall estate in Derbyshire being responsible for 13 miles of double-bank dry fly fishing on the Derbyshire Wye and its tributaries, all favourite haunts of Izaak Walton and Charles Cotton.

My teaching has led me to Germany, Holland and more recently to America as well as demonstrating at the British fly shows and game fairs.

Now, with countless trout and almost as many lost flies behind me, my greatest pleasure is to see the grin on a beginner's face after taking his first trout on a fly of his own making. Truly a magical moment never to be forgotten.

Introduction

Why, with so many books about fly fishing and fly tying, was I asked to write yet another one?

It was not because I am an expert, for I believe that no such thing exists. More probably it was because I can still vividly remember the multitude of things I badly needed to know about after picking up my first fly rod.

Although my whole life has been a matter of flies, feathers, trout and trout fishers, I am at best, what I would rate as an experienced beginner. Truth is, there is more to learn about the trout fishing game than can possibly be learned in a single lifetime.

I have approached the fly tying aspect by assuming a total lack of knowledge. The many books I read when I started always lost me somewhere along the line, simply because they blindly assumed I knew what they were talking about.

Rather than attempt a complete pattern guide, I have dwelt more on fly dressing methods and techniques. This is the way I teach and it seems to work.

I have tackled fly casting in much the same way and while there is no substitute for one-to-one instruction, I think that my analysis of the steps necessary for each kind of cast will enable the beginner to put out a reasonable line with a fair degree of delicacy to a rising fish. If I have succeeded, I will be a happy man.

Opposite: Philip White brings a trout to hand on the River Lathkill.

Their lifestyle

In the Northern hemisphere, trout spawn naturally during the winter months from November through to as late as February.

For successful spawning, they must have clean, well-oxygenated water and a river bed made up of a water-permeable mixture of gravel ranging from pea-sized particles through to quite large stones.

Trout instinctively know that fine silt is their enemy at spawning time, which is why they excavate their redds on the up-stream slope of a slight rise in the river where Nature ensures that the gravel is self-cleaning.

The egg-laden female carefully selects her preferred spot and digs out a shallow depression in the gravel by rolling on her side and undulating her whole body in powerful movements so that gravel rolls downstream. The hollow made to her satisfaction, she allows the attendant male, who was hovering above her while the hard work was being done, to approach the redd.

She arches herself so that her ovipositor, immediately in front of the anal fin, is low in the dip she has made and, with much quivering, lays some of her eggs whilst, at the same time the cock fish expresses some of his milt over them.

The water movement within the hollow is such that a proportion of the fertilised eggs are retained in the base until the female has moved upstream to cut another hollow at the top edge of the first, so covering the eggs. The process is repeated several times and it is noticeable that trout redds are most usually in the form of an extended oval.

Once she has completed her task, the hen fish withdraws to a quiet, deep pool while the cock fish goes off in search of another mate. As spring returns, the adults feed hard to recover their condition quickly since, by early May, the cycle has already begun again, with the next winter's eggs or milt forming within the body.

Meanwhile, the eggs slowly develop deep in the darkness of the gravel until they are ready to hatch in early to mid-March. They actually hatch in an imperfect form called alevins, relying on a yolk sac for the first few weeks of life which are still spent under the gravel. The developing fry work their way upwards, gradually venturing into the outside world by mid-May.

During the early to mid-1800's, it was discovered that it was possible to strip the eggs from fish by hand and that these could be fertilised, incubated in a stream and

Opposite: Brook Trout milling in a crystal clear stream.

Above: A veteran American fly fisher admires a new rod.

hatched quite successfully. The hatchery set-up used in those days varies little from that used almost anywhere today outside of the very large, specialised commercial hatcheries.

In artificial propagation, ripe cocks and hens are selected and the eggs and milt carefully stripped into a bowl. In the early days, this was done into a bowl of water but it was later found that the process was much more successful if the eggs were stripped into a dry bowl.

The discovery of the "dry method" is attributed to Russian M Vrasski in 1856, although it is almost certain that Seth Green, the famous American fish culturist discovered the process at the same time.

In this method, which I still use every year, the eggs are stripped from the hen fish first and then the milt from the cock fish is added. The mixture is carefully stirred to ensure full contact between eggs and milt and then the water is added and the mixture allowed to stand to allow the eggs to swell and harden.

I strip three hens and three cocks into a bowl at a time to ensure that all the eggs are covered by more than one source of milt, since one of the cock fish may be infertile. This way it is possible to save a complete bowl of eggs which could be wasted if the one to one ration is used.

Once the fertilised eggs are hardened they are carefully washed, decanted into hatching troughs and covered to keep them dark. Incubation takes about 70 days in my river, and about 35 days to reach the eyed ova stage, which is the point when the eyes of the growing trout can be seen through the shell.

At this stage, they can be handled quite easily and any dead ones picked out with a sucker tube. It is essential to keep the eggs in the dark right up to hatching, except when picking out the dead ones, and even after this, the young alevins need to be kept shaded until they are well onto the feed which is sometime in June. Once they have started to feed, it is possible to grow trout on for as long as required, for stocking into fishing waters or for the market.

Above: Eggs stream from a ripe trout.

The globe-trotting trout

*The Brown Trout is at home in Europe,
North Africa and all the way across to
North-western Asia whilst the Rainbow and
Brook Trout hail from North America*

To thrive, trout need relatively low water temperatures and well oxygenated waters. Transport them into these conditions anywhere in the world and they will quickly establish themselves as a breeding stock, provided there is adequate food stock.

During the second half of the 19th century, attempts were made to transport eggs to different parts of the world. Some were successful and had far-reaching effects on trout fishing the world over.

After several failures and research into chilling eggs with ice, both trout and salmon eggs were transported to Australia in 1862. Some 90,000 salmon and 1500 trout eggs were loaded into an ice-house filled with 30 tons of ice on to the ship Norfolk, ready for the journey from Falmouth in England to Melbourne in Australia.

The voyage took 77 days, but even then some of the eggs were sent onto Hobart in Tasmania where they were placed into specially prepared hatching beds in the Plenty River.

Four years later, the immigrants were spawning naturally in their new home, from where further strippings of eggs were taken and sent to other parts of Australia as well as onto New Zealand where they thrived and formed the basis of the trout fishing for which that country has become so famous. Sadly, the salmon did not fare well in Australia, despite their having established runs in a number of rivers and they disappeared after about 30 years.

While this pioneering was going on in England, Seth Green was working on the Catskill strain of the Brook Trout in his Caledonia hatchery in New York State and in 1869 sent some to England.

As well as Brook Trout, he worked with shad, Lake Trout, salmon and Whitefish and in 1870 took some shad fry to a hatchery in California which later returned the

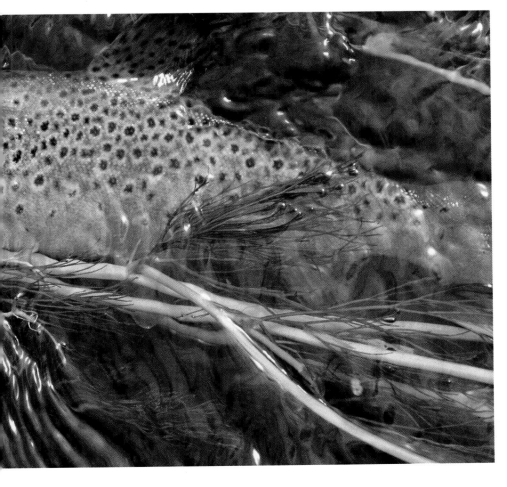

Left: An artificial mayfly proved to be too much of a temptation.

everywhere they have been introduced, the Rainbow has been a little less adaptable, especially in Europe where it does not breed very freely in the wild. Needless to say, New Zealand is a different matter, with a superb mixed species trout fishery.

The world is now a very much smaller place and eyed trout eggs are packed in cool boxes and flown across the world with ease, being in a spring fed hatchery thousands of miles from their original home in a matter of hours rather than weeks. It is also possible to keep hatcheries in full swing with rotations of eggs all year round.

Be that as it may, it was the development of fish hatching and rearing that allowed the spread of fly fishing to all parts of the globe so that the fishermen of so many countries could "angle to the trought..."

favour with a batch of "Mountain" Trout.

This was in 1875 and it was these fish that formed the basis for most of the eastern Rainbow Trout stocks in Europe, bearing in mind that he had already sent Brook Trout to England. In 1883, a consignment of Brown Trout arrived in the United States from Germany and were shared between Seth Green's hatchery and the one run by Fred Mather on Long Island.

For a great many years, the Brown Trout were known as Germans and Rainbows as Californians. Whilst the Brown Trout have adapted to breeding in the wild almost

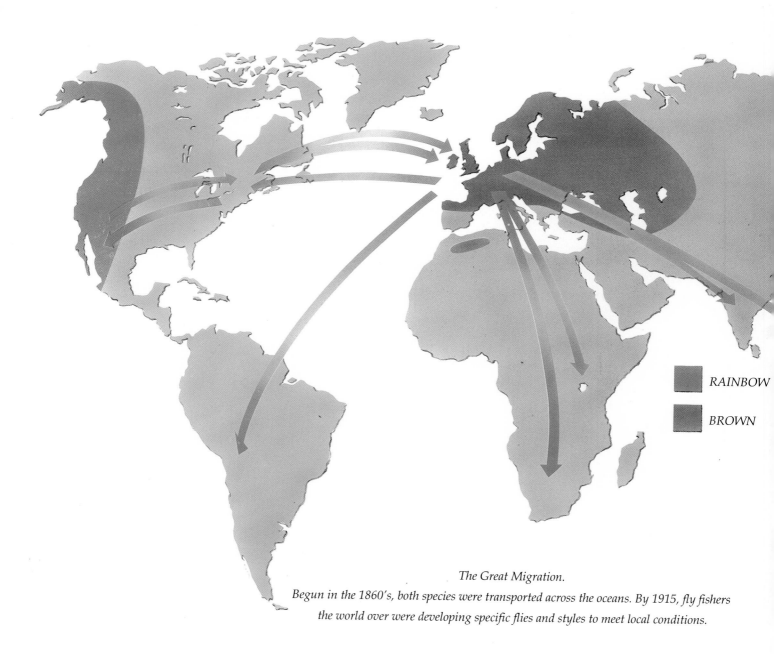

The Great Migration.
Begun in the 1860's, both species were transported across the oceans. By 1915, fly fishers
the world over were developing specific flies and styles to meet local conditions.

RAINBOW

BROWN

I am not too sure that this is a good thing as it introduces a degree of artificiality into what is essentially a field sport where the wild quarry is discovered, stalked and then taken for food in a highly pleasurable way.

Above: Trout eggs in the act of hatching.

The trout we catch

The Brown Trout is native to Europe and inhabits its rivers and lakes and those of North Africa and parts of Northern Asia.

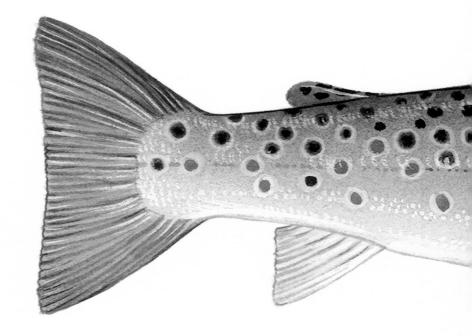

There are localised variations such as the Ferox, Gillaroo and Sonaghan, living in lakes in the British Isles which have specialist feeding patterns and display minute variations in their physiology as a result.

Scientifically included with the Brown Trout, the Sea Trout is merely an anadromous variation which I have deliberately left out of this book because fishing for it is normally different than for its land-locked cousins.

North America has three species, two trout and a char. The trout come from the western half of the country and are the Cutthroat Trout and the Rainbow Trout. Again, these species have local variations such as Paiute Trout, a kind of Cutthroat or the Apache Trout – a Rainbow – and include among the Rainbows a Golden Trout that scientists have tried to establish as a separate species.

In the eastern USA, the resident trout is in fact a char and is known as the Brook Trout and it was this fish that Seth Green first worked on and which was so popular in the very early days of the famed Catskill fishery. Again, for the same reasons as the Sea Trout, I have left out the Steelhead and other sea-going Rainbows.

Above: The Brown Trout.

Right: The Rainbow Trout (top).
The Golden Trout (middle).
The Cutthroat Trout (bottom).

All about fly rods

The first rods were simple affairs made from hedgerow saplings cut during the winter months, dried and then straightened and fashioned into fishing poles to which the line was directly attached.

From these first rods, the art of rod building progressed slowly to the heavy, but delicately tapered solid greenheart or lancewood rods made in England around 1840.

Even before this in the very early 1800's, people had started experimenting with a new material from Calcutta called bamboo cane.

The London firm of Higginbotham started to make rod sections from split cane at about this time but nothing much came of the venture. Only a few years later Samuel Phillippe from Easton in Pennsylvania started experimenting with two and three strip rods fashioned from the cane, and early rod maker Thaddeus Norris developed a four strip rod tip which he added to a rod with a butt made from

white ash and an ironwood mid-section.

By the late 1850's, Phillippe and son Solon, had developed a rod with a six strip cane tip coupled with a twelve strip butt of alternated cane and hardwood.

The cane strips were shaved into the round rather than being left in their usual flat section. In their pioneering footsteps came Charles Orvis of Manchester in Vermont whose factory, started in 1856, is still in production today.

Top: A Farlow rod circa 1872.
Above: Engraving on a lancewood rod.
Right: Fold-down rings on a Farlow lancewood rod.
Opposite: A selection of trout rods.

A decade or so later, Hiram Leonard, probably the best known of American rod makers came on the scene. His bevelling machine for cutting cane strips of constant uniformity was such an advantage over the competition that he kept it under lock and key for more than 75 years. Only his most trusted employees were allowed to see and use it.

Leonard also invented the waterproof ferrule and it was a Leonard rod that G. E. M. Skues referred to in his books as the W. B. R. or World's Best Rod.

In the 1870's Hardy Bros. of Alnwick re-established an English presence in the making of split cane rods and they soon developed an enviable reputation as rod makers throughout the world rivalling that of Leonard.

One of Leonard's workforce, Edward F. Payne, went out on his own in the mid-1890's and quickly became acclaimed for the quality of his craftsmanship, especially his reel seats which were undoubtedly in a class of their own.

His son Jim carried on the tradition, perfecting new techniques, one of which was pressing down the leaf nodes on bamboo strips with a hot iron rather than planing or filing which weakened them. Another innovation was flame-tempering and oven-curing the bamboo which considerably increased the power of the rod.

Many others played a part in the rod design story, not least of whom was famed

An ancient greenheart rod (left).
A Sharpes impregnated cane fly rod (right).

Opposite: Manicured trout stream perfection in France.

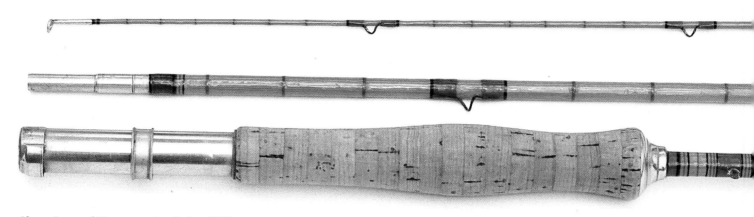

Above: Leonard Tournament rod circa 1905.

French hotelier and fly fisher Charles Ritz who collaborated with Payne in the design of his "parabolic action" fly rods. Another important name in the design of cane rods is Everett Garrison, who started making rods for himself during the late 1920's. Garrison lost his job in the Depression and became a full-time rod maker with a difference. A structural engineer by training, he set out to scientifically design the bamboo rod by analysing the physical properties of the natural bamboo.

Until then, rods were perfected by trial and error and relied on the instinctive "feel" that a true craftsman has for his material. Garrison not only worked out the tapers but also took account of the delicate balance between the cane's moisture content, the glue, rings, whippings, as well as the varnish.

The rods had what he called a "progressive action" which meant that the rod would respond in direct relation to the power used and that this power would reduce at an equal rate from the point where the rod started to flex, throughout the rod and down the line to the fly so that by the time the power reached the fly it had been reduced to zero. A long-winded way of saying that his fly rods were a joy to use.

Then it was discovered that Tonkin cane from Indo-China was harder than the Indian kind. Regardless of where it came from, split bamboo or cane rods held sway right until the early '50's, when tubular steel and then glass fibre came on the scene.

The steel rods did not last long but glass remained popular and was improved over

Left: Hardy Bros – rodmakers to the monarchy of Europe.

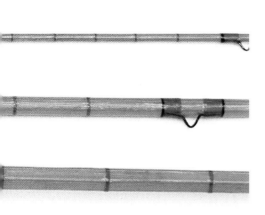

20 years until the Space Age hit us with a vengeance. Carbon fibre, or graphite, boron and kevlar became available to rod makers who had been struggling since the end of World War II to find a reliable source of top grade cane after China closed the Bamboo Curtain.

Most modern rods are tubular, but a couple of makers have returned to the old hexagonal shape preferred for bamboo

since it is possible to over-load any tubular rod to the point of collapse – as many long distance casters have found to their cost!

Rod length has gone full circle. In the mid-19th century rods were commonly ten feet or more and then gradually got shorter in length and weight until fishers such as Lee Wulff were extolling the virtues of little wands of around six feet. These are.now out of fashion, and rods are getting longer and longer.

Above: Detail from a Leonard rod.

Glass fibre fly rod (left).
Modern graphite rod (right).

Above: Hardy Hercules reel.

THE FLY REEL

Trout fly reels took longer to develop than the rod and little has changed in the design. True, they now have sophisticated clutch brakes and even multiplying gears, but in essence they are still the winch known by both Izaak Walton and Charles Cotton. Exactly who put the trout reel on the map is open to debate, but it has progressed through brass, Bakelite, gun metal, aluminum, to graphite.

Some of those early reels were beautifully made items and are much sought after by collectors, but their function is still to hold the line and sufficient backing whilst fishing and to provide a simple brake and winch function when playing a strongly running fish.

BELOW: An old brass reel.

Hardy Marquis reel.

Farlow's brass and Bakelite reel.

Hardy L.R.H. Lightweight reel.

An Army and Navy reel.

LINES AND LEADERS

Lines have come a long way since anglers were told back in 1662 how to select the horse hair for twisting into lines and casts as well as how to dye the lines to make them that much less visible in clear and coloured water, a problem that still perplexes today's fly fishers.

Over the next 300 years, dressed level silk lines were most used and as improved rod design brought longer casting lines, were tapered to improve their performance.

The double tapered, oil-dressed silk line was with us by the mid-1850's and ruled the roost for a century until plastic coated lines first made their appearance. These new tapered lines were coated with plastic instead of the oil dressing which quickly became sticky. The great leap forward came with the decision to add a "bubble" coating onto a level core, the taper being put into the coating. Much of this important work can be attributed to American fly fisher Leon Chandler.

The Forward Tapered line was originally developed for tournament casting about 90 years ago and has changed very little.

One development in the late 1950's that failed to catch on was the "self-loading"

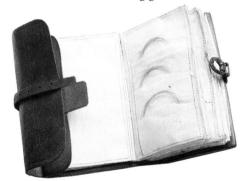

Above: Traditional British wet flies and some modern nymphs.
Below: Wallet holding gut leaders.

line. Called the Mallard, it soaked up water to give it enough weight to flex the rod. Although sound in principle, the weight was quickly lost during false casting.

As technology improved, weight was added to the line coating and it is this development that has most influenced fly fishing in the whole of its history, making accessible all the water depths available to the fly fisher for the first time.

STAYING COOL

Keeping the catch cool and fit to eat has always posed a problem. I firmly believe that the old-fashioned wicker creel takes some beating, with the woven bass bag coming a close second. Both can be submerged if necessary and both allow the air to circulate around the fish. The worst possible kind of bag is one made of plastic and it should never be used. Unfortunately, both the skills and raw materials for creel making are not readily available these days and they are expensive items.

Old wicker trout creel.

Choosing the gear

Irrespective of where you fish for trout, you
will need a rod, reel, fly line and flies.
Basically that is it, but as with all sports,
that is where the story only really begins.

The detailed choice of what gear you will use is dictated purely by the type of water and style of fishing needed to tempt the trout.

Graphite or carbon fibre rods are light years away from those made from hazel, blackthorn, bamboo and even whalebone used by our fly fishing ancestors.

I still prefer cane fly rods probably because I learned to fish with them as a boy, but sentiment must take a back-seat in favour of graphite.

Rod length is important and is governed by the kind of water being tackled and in extreme cases by the size of the fish that is expected to be caught.

The action of the rod, whatever its length must also be considered. Rod action can be divided into the three main classifications:

fast tip-actioned, those with a medium action with the main movement in the middle and top parts of the rod; and finally, those with a more gentle action where the action is throughout the rod's length.

Judging what rod to choose is difficult, especially for a newcomer.

For a small, tree-fringed stream and where you have to wade to get into casting range, then a rod designed to take four and five weight lines and with a medium to fast action and between seven and seven and a half feet long is the ideal tool.

On an open river or small lake, a medium to fast-actioned rod built to take four to six weight lines is the one to go for.

Bigger stillwaters often demand long distance casting and the rod must be man enough to cope with strong winds. Most

fly fishers who frequent these wide-water expanses rely on rods rated for seven and eight weight lines.

Fly fishers who prefer to fish in the traditional British style from a boat drifting along in front of the wind usually opt for rods at least a foot or more longer to present their small flies on lightweight leaders and five or six weight fly lines with utmost delicacy.

The big gun brigade who like to offer their often huge, feathery creations in the dark deeps use much stronger weapons built with the capability to hurl nine and ten weight lines towards the horizon.

All that said, the ideal for general all-round fly fishing is a medium-actioned nine footer rated for a six weight line.

Opposite: Fishing the evening rise on an Orkney loch.

PICKING THE REEL

Contemporary fly reels do not look all that much different from some of the very earliest invented, all of them working on the basic winch style. Inside however, modern reels are sophisticated affairs with all manner of brake systems using space age materials for checks and springs.

Whatever the construction, the reel is a line store whilst fishing and an asset when fighting a hard running fish. For these reasons, a good quality reel is an essential when fishing for trout large enough to strip off long lengths of fly line during the tussle. If smaller fish are the quarry then such a robust machine is unnecessary.

Whatever the size of the expected quarry, the reel must have an exposed rim for finger or palm control. If it has an adjustable drag or brake system, then so much the better.

Above: Reel with exposed rim.

FLY LINE TALK

The waterproofed silk lines ran a very long course until about 40 years ago. Still used by a dwindling band of traditionalists, their only real advantage over modern lines is their very fine tips which are often a help when presenting small flies with delicacy.

However, even this advantage is about to end with the rapid advances in the design of modern leaders.

Fly lines come in an ever-widening range of lengths and tapers. The ages old double tapered line is still favoured by many dry fly specialists. The weight forward lines and the specially designed tapers for throwing lures into the next county are the most popular.

Where once lines either floated or sank, now you can get lines in all sorts of densities in order to tackle a particular situation. There are those that barely sink below the surface and some that plummet to the bottom, with those that sink at different speeds in between.

All fly lines are rated in numerical order ranged from the lightest AFTM1 to a monster AFTM 15. Happily, this rating system is world-wide and was originally set up by the American Fishing Tackle Manufacturers to sort out a confusing jumble of different rating methods.

Basically, the rating stipulates a given weight for the first thirty feet of a line of a specific size so that a standard AFTM six weight line from any manufacturer, should correctly load a six weight rated rod for optimum performance. It is fair to say that both reputable rod and line makers can be relied upon to provide a well-balanced outfit of a chosen size.

For optimum fly presentation, it is a good policy to aim for the lightest suitable weight outfit in any fishing situation, but even the one-rod man can vary the outfit by having a range of lines to match the different fishing situations.

A double taper line traditionally provides delicacy of presentation; a weight forward line, which has all its weight built into the front part of its length, is ideal for both short line and medium range work for cruising fish; while the specialist shooting head outfit is the one to go for when the fish are feeding a long way off.

Whatever the profile of line, it must always be understood that for optimum performance, we must use a line one weight of line heavier than that for which

Above: A selection of different tapered fly lines.

the rod is rated. When thinking about shooting tapers then consider lines a couple of sizes heavier.

This may sound at odds with the AFTM line rating formula, but it is not really as it must always be remembered that the original concept was based on the old double tapered line.

Whatever the line being used, it has to be joined to the reel with a much thinner backing line which fills up the spare room on the reel drum and serves as a buffer should a strong-fighting fish strip away more than the thirty yards of fly line. A backing line can be twisted nylon, braided polyester, braided monofilament or of flattened solid nylon.

LEADERS AND TIPPETS

Left: Old gut leaders.

Modern nylons and polymers are incredibly strong and resistant to abrasion, although the pre-stretched filaments have a tendency to weaken at the knots. If you tie a careless knot in that stuff then you are in for a hasty parting with a hooked trout.

Some fly fishers prefer to make up their own leaders from different lengths and strains of nylon. Others prefer the off-the-shelf knotless tapers and a few are content to use a length of level nylon stripped off the spool.

There is no doubt in my mind that a well tapered leader helps present a fly delicately, but at the same time I have a sneaky feeling that they are perhaps not as important as we may like to believe.

Technology has also given us leaders fashioned from woven nylon in a wide variety of densities. The fly itself is secured to a very short, extra tippet of much finer nylon. I much prefer the tapered monofilament leader, either purpose made or home tied, from graduated diameters of nylon.

Until quite recently, tapered leaders were known as "casts" but the name has gradually dropped out of common use simply to differentiate between them and the physical act of casting the line.

The fine end of the leader onto which the fly is fastened is now known as the tippet. The spare spools most anglers carry for repairing or extending leaders, is known as tippet material.

While still dealing with leaders, it is perhaps as well to explain about droppers. Nothing confusing at all. They are just short lengths of nylon built into the leader at given points to take extra flies.

Getting into knots

Anglers have fought knee-deep in blood for centuries over the relative worth of the various knots and never more so than in the last 20 years with the introduction of ever finer and stronger nylons. It must have been quite a shock for those old timers to discover that their old favourites did not work at all well with more modern leader materials.

There are some old knots that work with nylon as well as with the old gut. One is the Double Overhand or Surgeon's Knot used to join together two pieces of nylon. It is a good knot for pre-stretched nylons but I am happier with the Four Turn Water or Cove Knot for normal nylons.

Another two from the old school are the Double Blood Knot used for joining two lengths of nylon and the Tucked Half Blood Knot used for attaching the fly to the leader tippet. A more modern knot for attaching the fly, the Non-Slip Mono Loop allows the fly more action whether it be dry fly, nymph, or even a large lure.

There are numerous knots for attaching the leader to the fly line. The simplest is to use a leader with a looped butt combined with a Sheepbend with the tip of the fly line. Clumsy it may well be, but it can often save the day if a pre-formed loop in the fly line fails.

Rather better is the loop formed in the end of the fly line, either by doubling back the tip and whipping a loop or adding a loop of heavy nylon using the Needle Knot or one of its variations.

The third alternative is to add a loop of braided nylon held in place with a fine tube. In all these forms, the loop in the leader butt is then attached to the loop on the end of the fly line.

The final way is to permanently fix the leader to the line with a Needle Knot. If a loop is formed at the end of the leader, the tippet section can be replaced very simply.

Loops are easily made with the Surgeon's Loop or the slightly more complicated Perfection Loop.

For attaching the backing line to the reel, I have never found anything at fault with either the Allbright Knot or the Stopped Double Overhand Knot.

DOUBLE HAND OR SURGEON'S KNOT

1. Lay two lengths of nylon together.

2. Make an overhand knot and pass through both ends.

3. Make two more twisting turns.

4. Hold both ends, moisten the knot and draw turns together.

5. The finished knot is ideal for joining lines of unequal diameter.

FOUR TURN WATER OR COVE KNOT

1. Lay two lengths of nylon together.

2. Form an open overhand knot.

3. Make three more similar movements.

4. Hold both pairs of nylon, moisten and pull knot together.

5. Ideal for adding droppers onto a leader. Always use the downwards pointing spur.

JOINING KNOT

1. Cross short ends of lines. Grasp the cross-over. Working from the left, twist one end around the line.

2. Fold ends together.

3. Change grip. Still working left to right, make seven turns with one end around the other.

4. Moisten and pull each spare end, then main line and spare ends again to bring knot turns together evenly.

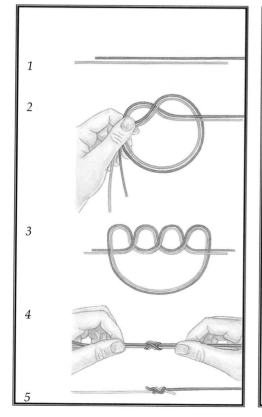

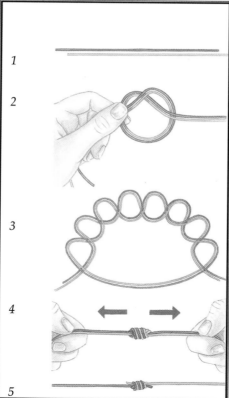

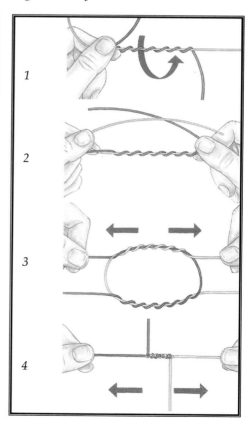

NON-SLIP MONO LOOP

1. *Form an overhand knot. Pass the ends through the hook eye and back through the open overhand knot.*

2. *Twist the ends around the main line three to four times.*

3. *Pass end through bottom side of overhand knot.*

4. *Hold fly and main line, gently pull the knot.*

TUCKED HALF BLOOD KNOT

1. *Pass line through the eye and make four turns around the main line. Pass the end through the gap next to the eye.*

2. *Take end through the open knot.*

3. *Holding the fly, moisten the nylon and pull the knot slowly to tighten.*

SHEEP BEND

1. *Pass the nylon through the loop, back around the main line and back again through the loop.*

2. *Take the nylon end around the leader and back again through the loose knot as shown.*

3. *Hold the main line and leader, slowly pull the knot turns together.*

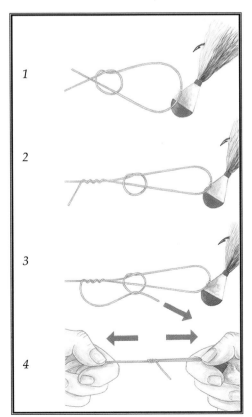

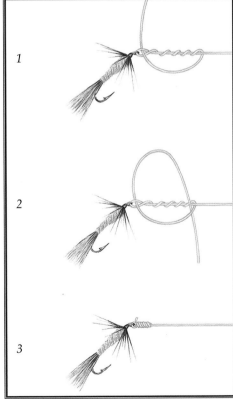

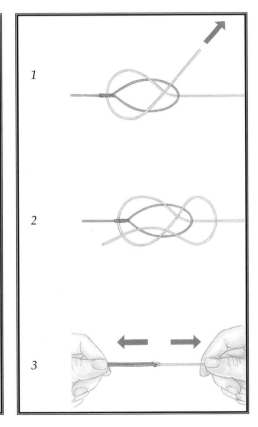

NEEDLE KNOT

1. Shave end of nylon to a long point.

2. Thread end through a large needle.

3. Push needle into fly line core and out through line half inch from the end.

4. Pull needle through.

5. Remove needle and pull six inches of nylon through line.

6. Lay needle on top with eye facing down the leader. Make six or seven turns around needle and fly line.

7. Thread needle and pull through underneath the turns.

8. Hold loose knot to prevent turns moving, pull the main line to tighten the knot.

SIMPLE LOOP TO LOOP

1. Pass one loop over the other, then insert the end through the loop.

2. Holding both lines, pull tight slowly.

SURGEON'S LOOP

1. Double the end of the line and pass the loop through forming an overhand knot.

2. Repeat once more.

3. How the knot should appear at this stage.

4. Pull loop and doubled nylon slowly to tighten the loop.

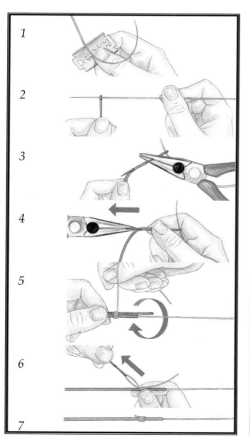

1
2
3
4
5
6
7

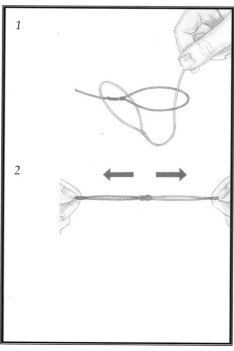

1
2

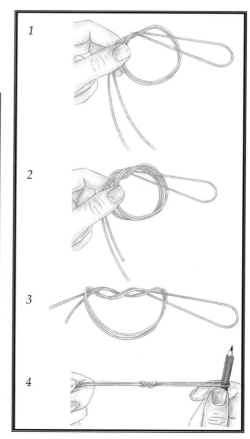

1
2
3
4

PERFECTION LOOP

1. Form overhand circle, having six inches spare.

2. Take spare end and pass over left thumb and back behind the first loop.

3. Place the spare end between the two loops, holding all in place with thumb and forefinger.

4. Reach behind and pull the second loop through the first one. Pull to tighten.

ALLBRIGHT KNOT

1. Pass nylon through loop on main line.

2. Working clockwise, make ten turns.

3. Pass nylon end through loop.

4. Pull nylon and main line to tighten knot.

5. Wrap spare end around leader and back through loose circle.

6. Pull waste end tight.

7. The finished knot.

STOPPED DOUBLE OVERHAND KNOT

1. Take end around reel spindle. Form an overhand knot around line.

2. Make overhand knot in the end of the line.

3. Pull knot tight. The overhand knot will stop it slipping.

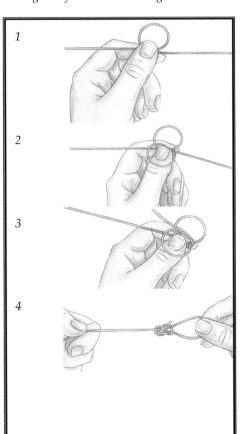

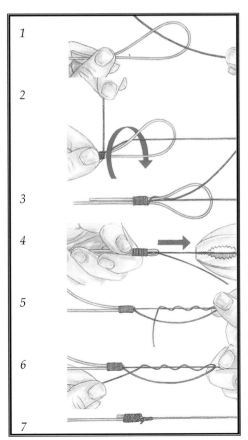

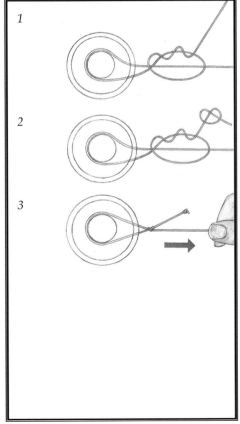

Presenting the fly

*Despite its being so fundamental to all that
we fly fishers do, the ability to cast well is
something rarely mastered. By that, I do not
mean simply sheer distance but
accurately and quietly.*

The competent fly caster must be able to control the line in the air from almost every possible position, from standing to kneeling and with the rod in all positions from the vertical to horizontal and on both sides of the body.

This ability is far more important than the hurling out of a fly more than 35 yards which in truth is something that very few fly fishers can achieve even with a shooting head outfit.

Casting performance purely and simply is all about controlling the loop of line in the air. The loop being the fly line in the act of rolling backwards and forwards in the air as you cast. This vital loop control is only possible if the movement of the rod tip is under firm control because the line will automatically follow the path of the rod tip in the air.

It is equally important that the rod should travel in straight lines, since any form of curve will bring loss of control in both distance and accuracy.

Timing and not brute power is the key to quiet, accurate casting and a few minutes spent watching a top-class caster will confirm this vital link all too clearly.

Casting a fly can be reduced to just two movements – the back cast followed by the forward cast with a pause in between.

Both back and forward casts are in fact accelerating movements that stop abruptly causing the rod tip to catapult forward transferring the power from the hand up to the tip.

Opposite: Casting to a rising trout.

Above: The standard 'thumb on top' grip.

THE GRIP

The best grip is with the thumb on top of the handle with the index finger slightly advanced to be level with and below the thumb, and with the other three fingers closed comfortably on the handle. This grip gives the strongest control on rod movements both back and forth since the thumb is the strongest digit on the hand.

Two other grips are commonly used but they are not really as strong. One is with the finger on top and pointing up the handle. The other is with the thumb and finger on either side of the handle. In both cases, there is much less control and power.

USING THE WRIST

The use of this joint is subject to more debate among fly casting instructors than any other, for it is the one that can make or break a good caster.

The wrist more than any other joint is the one that controls the loop made by the fly line in the air during the cast as does transferring the power from the grip to the rod tip. In essence, it puts the "snap" into the cast, but it must be under close control, giving a short, crisp flick at the very top of the back cast and the same again at the completion of the forward cast.

Too much either way, and the loop of line will unroll slightly "downhill", and the fly will hit the water both in front and behind the caster.

In years gone by, the beginner was often given a heavy book to keep under his arm throughout the casting stroke, a technique which created a very wristy stroke but which worked well enough for the normal casting distances.

Today, the whole arm is frequently used to simulate a throwing action but the wrist, elbow, shoulder and indeed the whole body has to be used with the rod rather than against it to cast really well.

THE STANCE

I recommend two stances for casting, one for accuracy, the other for distance.

For accuracy, it is better to stand with the right foot forward if right-handed, and the left foot forward if left-handed. The toe points at the target as well as the eyes and the rod hand. The nearest comparison is throwing a dart, and this stance is referred to as the Closed Stance.

For optimum distance, the left foot should be advanced if right handed or, again the contrary if left handed. In this stance, it is possible to cast from the feet upwards to get maximum and controlled power into the cast much like throwing a ball or javelin. It is important to keep the shoulders and chest well up in distance casting as in any throw, since any lowering will result in the rod tip dropping on the final delivery of the cast. This casting position is known as the Open Stance.

While casting is a practical skill best suited to practical instruction, I am going to attempt to pass on some tips and so it is perhaps as well to define one or two things before I go any further.

Casting is simply the act of propelling the fly line, leader and fly backwards and forwards in order to extend line and cover a target fish.

Loop is the term used for the line un-rolling backwards and forwards in the air as each cast is made.

Back cast is the commonly used term for throwing the line behind the caster and beginners are urged to keep it high to clear the grass and any bankside vegetation.

The front cast is the forward throw of the line, either to shoot line or to deliver the fly to the fish.

Shooting line is the act of allowing the line to slide forwards through the rings at the completion of the front cast either in the act of covering fish or to extend the length of line during false casting without actually letting it fall.

False casting is the continuous casting backwards and forwards, either of a dry fly that has become wet or, more often to extend line in the air in order to reach a particular fish or likely lie.

Above: The stance for accuracy.

Above: Feet positions when distance casting.

Casting the fly

Presenting the fly delicately to a trout is an almost poetical combination of hand and eye. The overhead cast, the first to be mastered, demands that the rod tip travels from the back cast into the front cast and back again in a straight line.

THE OVERHEAD CAST

When the rod tip travels in a straight line, the fly line unrolls in the air in the narrow loop which retains its speed.

Unfortunately, it has long been assumed that the elbow is the fulcrum of the cast, when logic shows that if this were so, the rod tip would have to travel in an arc pivoted at the elbow, this would produce a wide and uncontrolled loop which loses speed very quickly.

In reality, the pivot is the shoulder joint and the casting stroke is a complex set of movements in which the elbow rises and falls as well as opens and closes.

For accuracy, the rod hand must travel as close to the eye-line as possible and, as with any kind of throwing or punching movement, maximum power is achieved when the shoulder is right behind the hand. It is important then not to allow the elbow to go above the shoulder line and that the hand remain as close as sensibly possible to the body.

For distance casting, the Open Stance is adopted and power is applied over a much longer power stroke. The body swivels at the waist and hips and even the legs play an important part in applying maximum power.

The basic elements of wrist control and snap can be developed in a simple cast using the closed, accuracy stance. The rod is held with the tip pointing at the ground and then slowly lifted from the shoulder until the rod is in the 11 o'clock position.

The elbow is then brought into play and

1

2

3

4

5

6

the rod pulled back to the vertical. As the rod reaches this vertical position, the wrist is snapped back a little until the rod is inclined in the 1 o'clock position. A pause, and just as the line is unrolling at the end of the back cast, start to move the rod forwards, still held at the 1 o'clock position. Accelerate forwards at eye level and then snap the wrist forwards to the 11 o'clock position at the completion of the stroke.

Gently follow through while the line is unrolling in front until the rod is horizontal. It is most important that the power stroke from the 11 o'clock to the 1 o'clock position is made in a straight line so that a good loop is formed.

Throughout the cast, the left hand should remain low, around waist level and even lower at stage 6 so that the line is kept taut throughout the cast. Failure to maintain this tension results in a loss of power since the rod is not fully loaded.

THE OVERHEAD CAST

1. Start with the rod tip pointing down towards the water.

2. Lift, slowly at first, through stages 1 and 2 then accelerate through stages 3 and 4.

3. As the rod reaches the vertical, give a short, sharp wrist snap and stop the rod. Note the position of the upper arm at this point.

4. As the line extends, the rod drifts a little to the rear.

5. Just as the line is reaching full extension the front cast commences.

6. The rod hand drives forward at the shoulder level through stages 7, 8 and 9, where the wrist is snapped forward again sharply to complete the cast.

10. Once the power has been released into the line the rod gently follows through.

7   8   9   10

THE DOUBLE HAUL

This technique is used for distance casting and is the description of the motion used to speed up the line in the air. With a right handed caster, the double haul is performed by the left hand with the first haul on the back cast and the second haul on the front cast.

Each of these hauls is performed at the point of maximum rod flex just as the wrist snap is being applied at the completion of the stroke. At this moment, the line hand is pulled sharply downwards to about waist level and immediately raised to the rod hand again, almost as if on a piece of elastic, as the line shoots through the rings.

Most people can manage the one haul but have trouble with the second one.

The cure for this common problem comes from the top American casting instructor Mel Kreiger who recommends that the all-essential timing is best learned without a rod so that the rod hand is moved slowly backwards with an appropriate hauling movement of the line hand. Practising this dry run makes sure that the hand bounces back up to the rod hand immediately.

The rod hand then comes forward, then again, and the "Down-up" haul is made.

As far as I know Mel coined the term "Down-up" to describe the hauling motion

and it is the most apt description I have ever seen for the cast.

All of this mock casting is repeated in slow motion, at least, until the sequence is imprinted on the muscle memory. A spell of about ten minutes is enough to start before building up to full casting speed. Once the sequence is learned, it only takes a short time to put the double haul into practice with the rod.

The most common fault amongst casters is using several false double haul casts before the final release. This is sheer wasted labour. Get your timing right with practice and one, or at most two false casts are all that are needed for a good distance cast.

THE DOUBLE HAUL

1. Make one false cast backwards and then forwards so that the line is straight out in front with the rod and hand positions as in stage 1.
2. The rod and line hands travel back together until the rod is under maximum load.
3. Pull down with the line hand, and immediately allow the line hand to travel back up again to reach the rod hand as the backcast is completed in stages 5, 6 and 7. This is the 'down-up' movement already mentioned.
8. As the line straightens both hands are together.
9. The front cast is then made starting with both hands together.
10. The second downward haul is started.
11. The hauling hand moves downwards.
12. The downward movement continues.
13. The line is released.
14. The rod follows through to complete the cast.

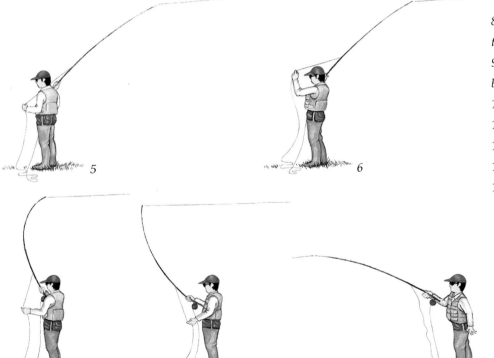

THE ROLL CAST

This is the cast needed to deliver a fly where there is no room for the usual back cast. It must not be performed with a chopping motion, which suggests a hard downward movement of the rod, but with a forward snap at eye level which lifts the line off the water as it unrolls forwards. Much more power is required with this cast and again, the wrist snap is vital. Since there is no back cast at all, the rod is lifted to the 1 o'clock position slowly and the line allowed to fall in a belly below the rod tip. It is driven forwards hard and the wrist snapped sharply to the 10 o'clock position.

THE ROLL CAST

1. Start with the rod pointing towards the water.

2. Lift slowly through 2, 3 and 4 so that the line glides across the surface. Cock the wrist slightly to take the rod tip even further back to form a large loop. Pause now, for it is this large loop that loads the rod for the cast and it must be allowed to form fully.

Some people make a full arm's reach to the rear to produce a bigger loop, but it is essential to bring the hand back again to the shoulder position, retaining the backward slope of the rod, before the front cast is made.

5. The forward cast is altogether sharper but shorter than in the overhead cast, almost like a good punch from the shoulder through positions 6 and 7 completing the cast with a smooth follow through.

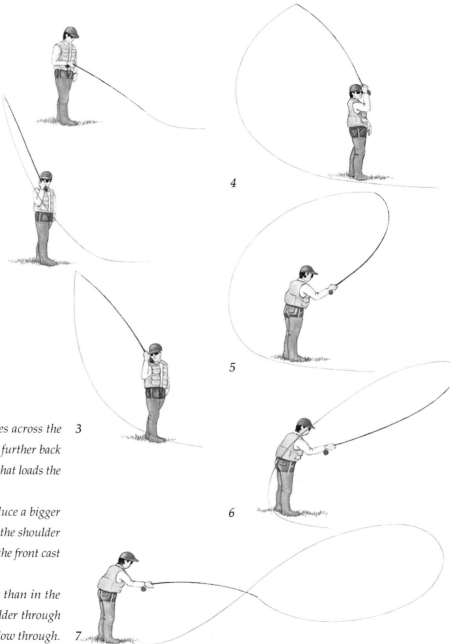

1

2

3

4

5

6

7

Some special casts

When fishing running water, it is essential to be able to cast a slack, or wavy fly line so that the fly can drift to a fish before it is whisked away by that old enemy we call drag. This menace can be overcome in several different ways.

THE HOLD BACK

When performing the usual front cast, it is normal to follow through after the power stroke is finished to give a nice straight line. If the rod is stopped abruptly without shooting any extra line, or the line is stopped early in its travels by gripping it with the line hand, the line will spring back a little and land like a wriggling snake on the water. The desired wavy line can also be achieved by following through on the forward cast allowing the line to almost reach the target and then to pull back towards you a little with the line hand.

Another way of putting in slack line is to wriggle the rod tip from side to side after the power stroke has been completed.

THE DROP

This simple little dodge means dropping the hand and pulling back slightly without actually applying any braking to the line. This release of energy opens the casting loop and gives the desired slack line.

THE REACH OR LEAN CAST

Again, after the power stroke has been completed and the line is travelling forwards, the caster leans forward or to the side with his arm outstretched so that extra line is laid well upstream. The line thrown should be straight from the rod tip to the fly and the caster then follows the line downstream with the rod tip to maintain the slack line for as long as is possible.

THE CURVE CAST

These are thrown with the rod approaching the side-cast position and are classed as positive and negative curves.

The Positive Curve, where the leader curls to the left for a right handed caster, is thrown with a tight loop and excessive power so that not only does the line straighten but curls both fly and leader into a return curve.

The Negative Curve is thrown with an under-powered and open loop so that it dies just before the leader fully unrolls. A small amount of slack given as the cast reaches its completion helps dampen down the power even further.

Dry fly ways

*The dry fly is fished to float on the surface,
imitating a freshly hatched fly, an egg laying
spinner or even an ant or grasshopper.
Despite its already being a recognised
method, it became the only "gentlemanly"
way to fish for trout among anglers on the
Test and Itchen during the Victorian era.*

The influential trio of Frederick Halford, George Marryat and Francis Francis probably did much to steer future thinking about dry fly fishing.

The chance meeting between Halford and Marryat in John Hammond's tackle shop in Winchester in 1879 was a landmark in British fly fishing. Their friendship led to a series of highly influential books written by Halford which rapidly became the established thinking on fly fishing.

Halfordian dry fly fishing was a formal affair, where only individual rising fish were cast to with an artificial copy of the natural fly and from a position downstream of the feeding fish.

On the well-keepered beats, trees were cut back away from the banks except as special features, but encouraged to grow a back-cast away from the water's edge to act as windbreaks and safe havens for insect life.

Bankside vegetation was encouraged but topped off at waist height, behind this the grass was mown to allow a quiet approach. Seats were positioned at intervals where anglers waited patiently for a fish to rise. Weedbeds were carefully sculptured to provide insect habitat and all was managed to suit the fishing of the dry fly.

Today, the upstream approach has been relaxed but, sadly, along with the decline in this strictly formal view of dry fly fishing, gone also are the water keepering skills that made it all possible.

Opposite: Philip White cutting weed on the River Lathkill.

Presenting the Dry Fly

The old military adage that time spent watching is seldom wasted is particularly true when fishing the dry fly. Before attempting to cast to the fish, no matter how eager you are, spend a few moments checking out the casting room both in front and behind. See if there are any fish between you and your target trout, which may be spooked by its companions rushing away, having been frightened by a fly line landing on their heads.

Simply, dry fly fishing involves the fly landing like thistledown above the fish's lie so that it drifts down over it like a natural fly.

If the fly lands heavily, or is dragged away by a contrary current, the alarmed trout will be put down. When you get it all right and the fish rises with confidence, give it time to turn back downwards before you tighten or you may well fail to hook it properly.

In the days when a noteworthy trout scaled no more than 2lb and the average fish barely half that, the advice to British anglers was to slowly say "God save the Queen" before lifting into the fish.

In the majority of waters, trout are very much larger these days and rather than attempting to invoke divine intervention in the demise of her Majesty, it is best to wait until the fish has turned downwards before making a positive move, even if it does take three times as long. I am certain that more fish are missed or lost in playing because of poor hooking by the strike being made too soon, rather than too late.

Read any book on dry fly fishing and there will be the dire warning not to let the fly drag on the surface. Good, sound general advice to follow – but not always, as there are times when adding movement to the fly can produce remarkable results, especially when fishing imitations of large flies and some terrestrials.

Sedges in particular are highly active creatures when hatching or when egg laying and imitations of this large fly are frequently given added movement, especially on the English stillwaters where retrieving them across the surface is a standard technique.

Far less often seen is the judicious use of movement on rivers, whether by tradition or not I am not sure, but if you watch the natural insects on the water, I think you will be surprised at just how many of them do move about on the surface.

Tiny flies do not create too much of a commotion, but flies like the mayfly, sedge, cranefly and stonefly really do make their presence felt. The usual way of adding this extra and obviously attractive movement is to draw in the line or to gradually lift the rod so that the fly skips across the surface, a technique often known as "skittering the fly". In running water, this causes a tight line and can lead to uncontrolled drag unless the fly is lifted off and re-cast. It also makes the fly produce a long wake, something to avoid as this rarely happens when the natural insect moves across the water.

I know of two ways of imparting the sought for short movement or even just a shiver to the fly, and both have greatly improved my own success rate with difficult fish. I spotted the first in the book "Fishing the Dry Fly as an Insect" written by Leonard M. Wright Jr. It entails casting positive and negative curve casts so that the belly of the leader is upstream of the fly. As the cast is fished out, the line is pulled back an inch or two so that the fly twitches just a little upstream. Wright specified the method for sedges but I have found that it works just as well when imitating other active flies.

The second way of inducing movement is what I call the shiver, and it is achieved by shaking the rod tip quite vigorously from side-to-side so that the motion travels down the line to the fly making it tremble, rather than drag on the surface which is bound to happen if the line is pulled. Try the dodge when imitating both emerger and spinner patterns, especially those of mayflies. It works.

Above left: A well-hackled dry fly.

Right: Offering a dry fly to a trout rising in a chalk stream.

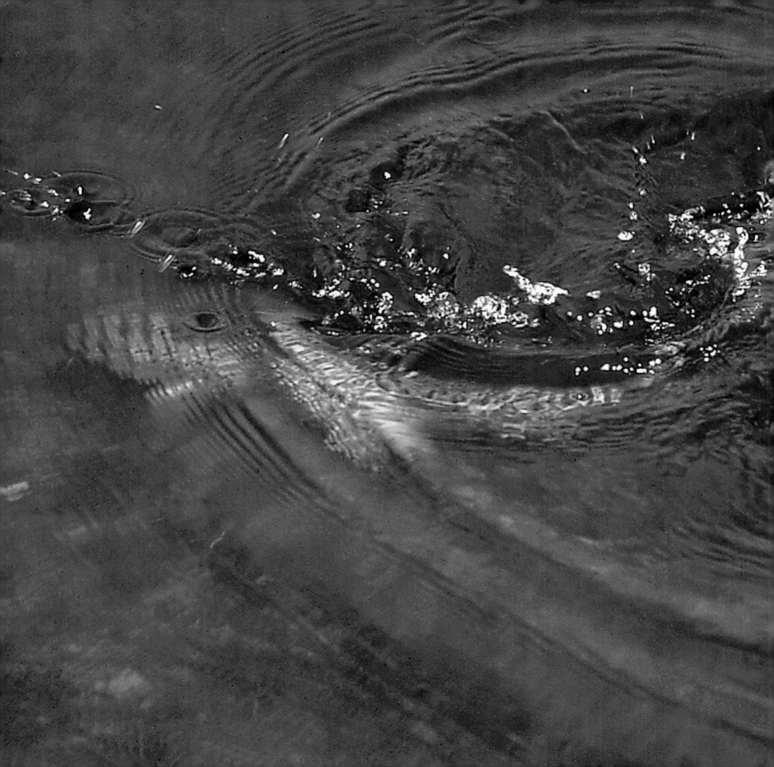

How trout rise

Trout rise to different insects in different ways and the swirl left on the surface after it sips in its chosen fly sends out all the necessary signals to a good dry fly fisher.

Usually, if the fish is feeding on the fully hatched dun, the fly can be seen and it is not unusual to actually hear the trout's mouth closing as it takes the insect. When this happens the only unknown factor is what species of fly is being taken.

This knowledge is vital as trout can be highly selective at times, ignoring more easily seen insects for far less obvious creatures. The other obvious type of rise is the hard slash trout make at large flies such as a mayfly, sedge or crane fly, all flies that signal their presence on the water by their futile thrashings.

The most difficult rise to decipher with accuracy is the gentle sipping rise where the trout sits almost at the surface and just tilts enough to sip in the insect off the surface. The chosen insects trapped in the sticky film can be spent, emerging, or crippled flies or terrestrial insects such as aphids and ants unlucky enough to be blown onto the water.

During the day, this puzzle is not difficult to solve as it simply means taking time out and watching the surface. Never try to solve the problem by going through the fly box, trying this fly for a few minutes and then another as this only serves to put the fish down altogether.

The one time when this sage advice can be ignored is during that magical hour at twilight when it seems that every trout in the stream is busy sipping insects off the surface and you cannot identify the chosen item highest on their menu.

It could be a spinner, emerger, upwinged fly or sedge - but who cares? You cannot see well enough to change the fly, neither will you have the time to chop and change before the frantic rise suddenly stops, so you must fish on with faith pinned firmly on the fly you have on the end, with all your senses straining to even see where it is on the water, lifting into every rise in the hope it was your fly that was chosen. Just now and again you are right. This is dry fly fishing at its very best.

Above: Landing a trout at twilight.
Opposite: Turning down after taking the fly.

Fishing the wet fly

Thought by many to be the easiest form of fly fishing and scorned by the disciples of Halford and his followers, fishing the wet fly in a stream is a style honed to an art form in the mountain and moorland streams of Great Britain, Europe and North America.

The flies developed for this style are in two distinct forms but a lack of wings is common to most of the flies in either style. Why they differ so much is hard to say but it is likely that the regional water conditions dictated their form. Some streams are rough and full of boiling pots and holes, and on these the bushy, hard hackled and spiky-dubbed fly reigns supreme, whereas on the wider, smoother streams, a slim, soft hackled and thinly dressed fly is more favoured.

A look at the flies used in Britain for centuries gives an insight into the reasons behind their design.

Those from the English West country and Wales have stiff, long fibred gamecock hackles and herl or dubbed bodies. There are still large natural flies on these streams but the fishing method also had a big effect on their make-up. Both styles favour hackled flies rather than those with wings, but why there is such a wide gulf between the two is difficult to define though it is possible local fly life had a strong influence. Certainly, the majority of the West country and Welsh rivers are rough and tumbling, dotted with little calmer pockets, while the more northern rivers are larger and flow more sedately.

These bushy flies are cast into pockets, and are frequently fished downstream to make the stiffish hackles protest against the flow to give the impression of a living insect struggling for survival. The casts are usually short, as are the drifts allowed for each cast, and more life is imparted to the

Left: A leach of traditional English wet flies.
Right: Tiny flies from the wild Scottish
Border country.

fly by tweaking the rod tip. The wet fly game in these tumbling places is a pocket picking, totally absorbing affair which demands keen eyes and lightning reflexes. A method to be scorned by the dry fly disciple – not a bit of it!

The English North country and Scottish Border style of fly is very different, being much smaller in general and thinly dressed with soft mobile hackles designed to flicker with the illusion of life in even the slowest of flows. These little flies closely imitate the emerging and drowning insect, but instead of fishing the quieter pockets between strong flows and boulders, they are fished in a longer drift over gravelly or rocky runs so that the current plays through the hackle fibres even as the fly drifts naturally downstream without any additional movement imparted by the angler.

The fishing style for these flies is frequently known as the Downstream Method, a misleading term which has led to the flies being cast downstream and allowed to drift around to the angler's own bank.

This is definitely not the most effective way of fishing these flies. The correct approach to downstream fishing is to start at the top of the stretch and to cast the flies, usually in a team of three, upstream and across so that they drift along with the current for some distance until well below the angler where they will start to drag. Then they are lifted off and cast upstream once again.

When the run has been fished out, the angler takes a couple of paces downstream and the next lie or run is fished in the same way. It is this continuous downstream movement by the angler that gives the method its name and not the direction in which the flies are fished.

In lower water flows and when there is a hatch of flies, it is more common to fish from the lower end of a stretch in an upstream direction, casting a short slack line into every likely hole and behind every stone or obstruction where a feeding trout may be lying.

Spotting the takes

Whereas in dry fly fishing the take can be seen as a rise form, the same cannot be said about fishing the sunken fly. For many, the first indication of a take is a tugging at the rod top usually associated with a missed fish but there are a good many ways in which takes can be registered before this happens.

The very first requirement is total concentration. If you want to watch the birds and flowers, then lay the rod down. If fish are taking close to the surface then you will spot some sort of disturbance in the form of a swirl, a hump in the surface, a slight flattening of the surface in a ripple or the wink of a fish's side as it turns to take the fly.

If the wind or roughness of the stream prevents you from spotting these obvious signals, then you must watch for any unnatural movements of the line or leader. The lightest twitch or halting of the leader where it enters the water should be met smartly with an instant lifting of the rod. It may be that the fly has just touched a weed but more often than not the result will be a trout.

If water or light conditions are poor, attach a small indicator between fly line and leader as a visibility aid. Bite indicators are nothing new by any means, as they were used a century ago. Not the fancy fluorescent wools or floating poly beads of today but mere scraps of natural sheep's wool plucked from a hedge. The use of indicators is frowned upon by some fly fishers as being just a shade above cheating and I must admit to not thinking too highly of them in the past. However, my eyesight is not what it was and my opinion is rapidly changing.

When the trout can be seen, watch its mouth or the way the fish moves as it closes on the fly. When a trout opens its mouth it shows white, so if you spot the flash of white, lift the rod immediately.

Above: Presenting a wet fly.

If you are not close enough to watch the mouth, then study the fish's movements and react smartly to anything that does not look quite right, such as a sudden lift in the water or a slight turn away from its normal position. A fish will move from its position at an angle to the current, then straighten as it takes the food item before swinging back to its normal post. Lift the rod quickly when the fish straightens, for if you wait until it turns, you will probably be too late to make a firm contact.

River nymphing

Fishing the nymph is a natural progression from the old North country wet fly style and includes many of its techniques. Fishing the nymph has been credited to G. E. M. Skues in particular, and it is certain that he recorded much of the early work.

Skues took the old northern flies and adjusted their shape very slightly to give a pronounced thorax. He added tails where there had been none but continued to fish them in the same way.

He certainly upset an awful lot of people in the process and it was quite some time before nymphing became an acceptable way of fishing for trout.

Although Skues did include a shrimp imitation among his many patterns, it is generally accepted that it was Frank Sawyer who perfected the weighted nymph techniques so popular today. Sawyer's own simple patterns, dressed with just copper wire and feather fibres or even darning wool, were designed to sink quickly to bottom feeding fish and to be cast upstream above spotted fish and then

Above: The Snipe and Purple is still a firm favourite on England's northern trout rivers.

drifted naturally past them.

The heavy nymph is sometimes brought to life by a little pull on the line or a lift of the rod tip as it approaches the trout. This

sudden movement often induces the fish to instinctively grab the morsel.

In the right hands the "induced take" is lethal, even in places where no fish can be seen, but the method's real secret is in recognising the take as the fish either opens its mouth or swings sideways to intercept the fly.

All sorts of indicators are used to help spot these lightning takes from little cork bobbers, fold-over foam pads and even slips of fly line covering slid onto the line tip. Some are designed to hold the nymph at a pre-determined depth but I do not accept this as pure fly fishing since a form of extra terminal tackle is used instead of skill on the part of the angler.

Fishing the loch style

Fishing in the loch style goes back 200 years and more to the days when tackle did not lend itself to long casting and where fishing in lakes was done almost exclusively from a drifting boat.

The rod was tackled up with a cast of three or more flies and the boat set to drift before the wind. The angler cast his flies in front of the boat on a short line ten yards long or even less and fished them back by slowly lifting the rod and gathering in the line.

As the rod neared the end of a long slow lift, the top fly was bobbed along the surface to imitate a struggling insect and to this day the top dropper fly is known as the bob fly. If the trout followed the dancing fly but refused to take, the line was gently switched forwards into a Roll Cast and the cast fished out again.

Modern names for this ancient technique include "over the front" or "shortlining", both apt descriptions of the simple but highly effective method.

With the introduction of competitive fishing on major British stillwaters, the old style has advanced in leaps and bounds. On an overcast day when the trout are active on or near the surface, it is probably my own favourite way of taking stillwater trout, but now my old boxes which are filled with traditional flies of yesteryear have been put aside in favour of more modern imitations of the nymphs and flies found on stillwaters.

Special techniques have evolved to cope with the bad weather conditions often experienced on the larger lakes. Now regarded as a standard part of a boat fisher's gear, the drogue makes the method perfectly possible on the roughest days when the waves are high. A drogue is simply a form of sea anchor that works like

Opposite: Drifting along on a Scottish loch.

an underwater parachute in the water slowing down the speed of the drift.

Once the province of the floating line, loch stylers now use all manner of density lines to present their flies at all the many different depths.

Boats can be trimmed to drift at an angle to the wind by careful positioning of the drogue on the side of the boat of the angle of the rudder or outboard engine and even by adjusting the position of the anglers in the boat.

The speed of the drift can also be slowed down if the narrow end of the boat is presented to the wind rather than the full length of the more usual sideways position.

GOING FOR THE DEEPS

Todays modern fly lines have made it possible to fish the large lakes and stillwaters at all depths and it is common for anglers to anchor over a known hot-spot and to fish it hard with every sort of density line from a floater to a very fast sinker.

Using a system of counting, or even a stop watch, the angler can discover the level at which the fish are concentrated and then to fish at this depth with every subsequent cast. This may be as much as 40 feet down and fishing at depths like these is a very specialised style calling for the utmost patience, if only in the wait for the line to sink down to the discovered feeding layer.

It is not a style for everybody, but it does produce some very large trout which would probably not have been caught by more conventional ways of fishing closer to the surface.

Left: Deep fishing on a small stillwater.
Opposite: Boats gather over the deeps.

Stillwater bank fishing

This branch of the sport has probably received most benefit from developments in fly rods and lines because it has put more of the water within the angler's reach.

In the early days of stillwater fishing it was common to see anglers using double handed salmon rods to cast any real distance. Today, a competent caster using a nine foot six inch rod and a shooting head will put his flies and lures 40 yards and more into the lake with ease.

Unfortunately, stillwater anglers with a quest to put their flies far out into the lake have a tendency to wade out from the shore. Rather than put them in closer contact with more fish, wading has the opposite effect, driving away those trout swimming close inshore to a distance out of reach of even the most prodigious caster.

The bottom line is that even on really large stillwaters, stealth coupled with a good knowledge of the lifestyles of both fish and fly life, will produce more fish than a blind reliance on sheer casting brawn.

Perhaps nowhere is this basic truth more apparent than on huge stillwaters such as England's 3,000 acre Rutland Water or the even larger still sheets of water like New Zealand's Lake Taupo which is almost 250 square miles in area.

The sheer size of a large stillwater overawes most first time visitors. The truth is that they need have few worries about the sheer size of the fishery, as many trout will be found close to the bank, provided of course that the area has a good food supply and has not been disturbed too much by anglers who have gone before them.

These basic requirements, coupled with weather conditions, always dictate trout behaviour in any water.

There is no substitute whatever for local knowledge on large stillwaters since it is possible to work out in advance of the visit where the trout are likely to be found in numbers and what they are likely to be feeding on.

Prevailing winds, hatches of certain types of fly or migrations of forage fish like roach fry and smelt all play their part in deciding a trout's feeding habits. No rule book will ever be a substitute for local knowledge, but it is something that is hard earned.

If you do not know a water well then it is a wise move to head for a bank with the wind blowing parallel to it, especially if the shore has a series of small peninsulas along its length where the wind and wave action stir up the bottom encouraging fish to feed close inshore.

Weedbeds, sunken hedges and other

features are important fish holding areas. Taking a look at the lie of the land around the water will also give helpful clues as to where to fish. Shallow areas will usually be where flat land runs to the water's edge. It follows that areas of deeper water within casting range will be at the bottom of steep sloping banks.

Right: Watching and waiting for the trout to start rising.

Stillwater flies

In the main, what flies will be used depends on the water quality. I find that dark flies do best on acid waters and I have a liking for flies with dark claret, black and peacock herl bodies in this kind of water. On the richer, more alkaline fisheries where the fishery is rich in fly life, I have a fondness for flies based on soft olives, browns and yellows.

Flies dressed with hare's fur seem to be acceptable wherever they are fished.

Flies designed to imitate small fish are used with great success in the richer waters where forage fish abound in their millions and stillwater anglers always need to carry a greater range of patterns than any other fisherman.

In the 1960's the rage was all for brightly coloured attractor flies, but recently, stillwater fishers have taken a more imitative approach and there is no doubt that they are reaping the rewards for this more thoughtful approach.

Fly fishing in stillwaters needs some sort of retrieve and it is all too easy for the newcomer to carry on regardless using the same old retrieve irrespective of the prevailing conditions or even of the style and size of fly he is offering.

In my early days as a fly fisher, I met an old chap who always caught his fair share of trout. This was in the late 1960's when lake flies were of the attractor type rather than imitations of any living creature. Rather than just retrieve them in the usual mechanical way, he told me to pull them to the rhythm of an old British army marching song which produced a mix of short and long pulls.

Whilst I do not advocate retrieving flies to music, I suggest it as a reminder to keep varying the speed of the retrieve.

What worked yesterday may well not do anything at all the next and it is not uncommon to find a large lure and a small nymph being fished on the same leader and being pulled at a steady two feet a second.

This is not all that quick for a fish imitating lure, but rocket-like for the nymph. Just a little thought would suggest that the nymph should be fished slowly.

Failure to understand these basics can lead to many fish turning away, or taking little plucks at the flies.

Takes are not always all that easy to spot in stillwater unless the trout actually grabs the fly and hooks itself in the process, something that happens far more often than we care to admit.

Never forget that the angler who always catches more than you is not just lucky, he just works harder. From the moment the flies land on the water they are fishing, and you must be ready for even the slightest movement of the line and of the water around the line and flies.

Opposite: The end of a perfect day on an English Rainbow lake.

Even when fishing a well-sunk fly, it is essential to keep both hand and eye contact with the line at all times ready for that slight pull from a taking trout.

It is amazing how many fish pick up a fly, sample it and reject it again without the angler ever having even an inkling of what is happening. Indeed, I am sure that all fly fishers would benefit from a day or two on a river without a rod.

Takes that occur like this are known as On the Drop for obvious reasons and are most common when imitative or nymph patterns are being used, so be specially aware when using these sort of flies.

Left: A chalk stream nymph fisher's box.
Opposite: Casting to trout feeding on tiny
midges.

Fishing small stillwaters

This is really a quite new aspect of our sport with new trout fisheries being created from old quarries, gravel pits and quarry workings. Such has been the demand for this kind of fishing that many fisheries have been specially created from productive farm land.

Probably the best known small water in England is Two Lakes in Hampshire, a model fishery started just after World War II by Alex Behrendt.

These little fisheries provide fishing for often very large fish in a very controlled way, with fresh fish being introduced on a regular, sometimes daily basis. They are usually spring or stream fed with gin-clear water, a factor that has led to the development of specialist stalking techniques and it is here, as with clear water nymph fishing on the streams, that the ability to spot a lightning take spells the difference between success and failure.

The most popular method among these highly successful anglers revolves around the ability to cast a heavily weighted nymph a short distance with pin-point accuracy and then to spot and react to takes that rarely involve any acceptable movement of line or leader. All you see is a slight quickening of the gills or a glimpse of white as the fish opens its mouth.

Fish that survive those initial first few precarious hours after release when they are prone to investigate every morsel of potential food with fatal results, can be-come extremely difficult to catch and the ability to stalk, or stand heron-still, is a must if you are to outwit a wary veteran. If the water is not clear, it is essential to watch the fly line or the leader butt for any unusual movement which indicates a take.

Flies for this specialist style are usually imitative patterns based on shrimps and other creepy crawlies, but some fish are taken each day on bright flies.

No special tackle is needed for this kind of fishing but always take a net that is large enough to take a good sized salmon. These small water Rainbows can grow very large indeed and the thought of trying to get a 20lb plus Rainbow Trout into a net designed to engulf stream-sized fish is not worth thinking about.

Above: One damsel nymph too many.

Opposite: A good Rainbow nears the waiting net.

The etiquette of the game

Gaining a rare sense of solitude and contentment is far more important than catching huge numbers of fish. On wild streams this presents no problems but it is on waters shared with others that etiquette becomes such a vital ingredient of the game.

It is the unwritten rules, not those printed on your permit, that make our sport such a pleasurable recreation. The last thing any fly fisher needs is to have someone else crowding his space.

If you are catching fish when others arrive, move on after the next fish unless the fishery rules say otherwise.

If someone is already fishing a pool, either follow him up or down at a proper distance, or better still, wait until he pauses to change a fly or net a fish before telling him that you are going to start fishing.

In a boat, watch your drift so that you do not cut across someone else's "water" and always observe caution when moving station so that you do not ruin another boat's sport by getting too close.

All these simple "rules" are really based on common courtesy. A smile costs nothing and simple manners and pleasantries will often soften the heart of the most hardened fishing hog. Of course, there will always be those who seem incapable of thinking about others or recognising good manners when they see them.

Left: Fly tackle, ancient and modern.
Opposite: Peace and solitude.

Women in flyfishing

*"The best chum I ever had in fishing was a
girl, and she tramped just as hard and fished
quite as patiently as any man I ever knew."*

So wrote Theodore Gordon in 1865 and although the lady's name was never disclosed, Gordon remained a bachelor after she apparently left him "...... very disappointed in love."

Since fly fishing history really started with Dame Julyans Berners, it is proper that I should perhaps clarify a point. Throughout the book, I have used the masculine gender when talking about fishermen, not because I am chauvinistic by any means, but because it is the accepted English of my generation.

Whilst there are not that many lady anglers, those I have met are all good fishers and some are exceptional. Their success has recently become the subject of a book which attempts to pin down their remarkable successes onto their hormones

Above: Proof enough of this lady's skills.

*Opposite: A lady fly fisher subdues a lively
stillwater Brown Trout.*

presumably exuded onto the fly as they tie it to the leader. True or not, lady anglers often prove that they have that extra touch.

As an instructor, all I have to say is that women anglers are much easier to teach than men. Those I have taught have been far more receptive to advice and all have shown a degree of determination not shared by many male anglers.

The same goes for fly dressing, but not because of their smaller, more nimble fingers. Indeed, some men with huge hands are able to produce the most delicate of flies imaginable. As for the quality of the fruits of the vine, those produced by both sexes are on a par.

What do trout see?

For decades, it has been accepted that trout have extremely good eyesight. The position of its eyes suggests that it can see really well in a huge arc from very near its tail right around the front and to very near the tail on the other side.

Down its sides, the vision is monocular but at the front, a trout has very sharp binocular sight. From behind, the fish is virtually blind and has to rely on its other senses, a serious disadvantage as I have proved many times by tapping a trout on its tail with a rod after a stealthy approach.

Not only does a trout enjoy good vision under water, it has the added advantage of wide-angled sight into the air. Most fly fishers are familiar with the trout's cone of vision as well as its reliance on the mirror effect from the underside of the surface.

Of the two, I am convinced that the mirror effect is by far the most important. If we look at the cone of vision in the usual way, we know that the light rays from above refract as they pass through the surface to such an extent that a trout can see down to within 10° from the surface. This explains why a trout is triggered into taking a fly, since any object standing above the surface will appear top first into its sight as it approaches the base of the inverted cone. This fact has prompted great debate on the relative values of flies with and without wings.

It may well be the deciding factor, but I firmly believe that the mirror plays a most important role in triggering the initial response from the trout.

Look at any mirror or a pane of glass and the first thing that strikes your eye is a slight spot or blemish. Apply this to a trout and think what a tiny insect does to that mirror. I think it goes even further than that, with the trout being perfectly able to recognise the various "footprints" left by the different kinds of insects.

This is what sets off the response, the appearance of the insect's wing in the cone of vision rubber stamping its final evaluation.

There is also, I think, a third trigger and one which is often ignored when fishing a dry fly, and that is movement. I do not mean the exaggerated skating motion put in by some fly fishers, but tiny movements made by the natural fly as it slides from its shuck and dries on the surface. In the case of land born insects, the movements come from kicking legs and buzzing wings as it tries to escape from the water's grip.

Opposite: A trout's-eye view of an angler.

If you look really closely, even small flies create minute rings on the surface. Put vision, the mirror effect and movement together and you have discovered the routine that a trout takes whenever it feeds from the surface.

Underwater too, there are similar sight triggers, the most important being shape, colour and movement, but in which order of importance we should put them I am not sure. Usually, matching the size of the natural insect will bring the hoped for response, but there are times when a larger than life artificial will provoke more interest although I personally prefer to match size for size whenever I possibly can.

I also believe that shape plays a vital role and my imitative patterns are all tied with this much in mind. Colour is a far more complex issue.

I think they can see colour, not in the same way as we do, but see colour they most surely do. We have all had the experience of a trout that has steadfastly ignored a fly only to take one dressed in exactly the same way and of the same size but in a different colour.

I recall one such instance very clearly when fishing during a hatch of midges on a stillwater. After just the one half-hearted

Above: A spent mayfly.

pluck to teams of red and black buzzers, my wife and I packed up after dark only to hear that other anglers had caught trout after trout on a claret version, even into the dark. Had it not been for the way that sound travels over water at night, I would have gone away totally ignorant of just how close, or how far, I was from having a really good evening's fishing.

Compare red, black and claret in near darkness and then tell me that trout cannot distinguish different colours!

Another indicator that they can tell the difference are the colour changes that trout go through during spawning. As a teenager, I fished a river that was not renowned for its fly fishing where most trout were

caught with minnows and worms. My own favourite method was a lip-hooked minnow, free-lined in among the weed beds. At spawning time, the male minnows became very striking, so much so that we called them Soldier Minnows. At this time, the trout showed a marked preference for the dull-coloured females, often ignoring the brighter male minnows altogether. What was most annoying was that the hen minnows were difficult to trap, presumably because they had other things on their minds at the time.

I can only assume that the trout favoured the females because they were carrying eggs, something not unheard of when fishing prawns for salmon which very often much prefer an egg-laden bait.

Whatever the reason, it would seem that the trout must be able to distinguish between male and female minnows by colour, especially when slashing into the milling shoals on the shallows.

Opposite: A modern emerger pattern giving off all the right signals.

How a trout thinks

As a good deal of my time as a river keeper is spent watching rather than trying to catch trout, I perhaps see the fish from a different angle to the fly fisher.

Trout are both predator and prey, with highly developed senses of sight, sound or vibration, smell and an acute awareness of anything unusual either in or out of the water.

Fish have been on this earth a lot longer than humans and have built-in safety alarms that we have either lost or perhaps never possessed. Scientists frequently denigrate trout as having a small brain incapable of learning even the simplest of lessons, but do they really need a large brain in order to thrive and survive? They do not need to drive a car or use a word processor. Perhaps without large brains we could learn to live in harmony with Nature rather better than we do.

Fish need a brain capacity sufficient to eat, sleep and avoid capture long enough to reproduce themselves, all memory skills aided by a very sophisticated set of senses.

Two things guaranteed to put the trout to flight are movement by the angler, rod and line, their shadows and the flash from the rod when casting.

The flash question first. If we can see the flash given off a rod and light coloured line from half a mile away on a sunny day, is it any wonder that trout will very often dive for the nearest cover at the first wave of a rod or the flicker from a fly line even when there has been no shadow thrown by either. A sound enough reason I would have thought for using matt finished rods and a dark or dull fly line, all factors out of favour with the tackle makers who rely on cosmetic appeal to sell their wares.

The line colour argument has raged for years, some experts basing the choice of a light coloured line on the fact that the underside of a warship is harder to spot from underwater if it is painted white and that many fish-eating birds have white bellies. There is a serious flaw in this line of thinking and that is the exclusion of movement. Add motion to a gannet or a white fly line and you have produced a danger signal that causes fish to take evasive action. The gannet of course overcomes the problem with sheer speed, something we cannot possibly reproduce in a fly line.

All movement from above presses the panic button, understandably, since many of their enemies come from above and so it is natural for them to dart into an area of shadow.

Opposite: Rising to olives in a Hampshire chalk stream.

Right; Heavy-duty leaders by Hardy's.

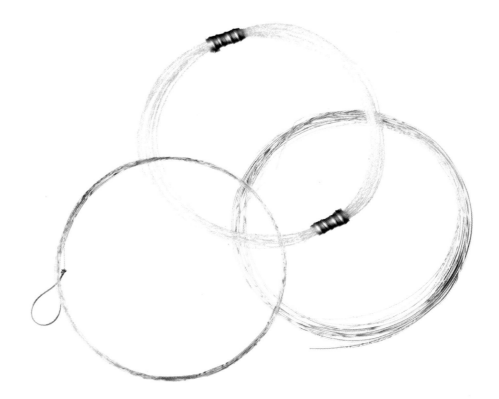

Watch the reaction of a fish when even a crow's shadow touches the water. Panic. It instinctively turns and dives for cover even before it really assess the situation, and while some will start to feed immediately, others will flee for cover.

In days gone by, river keepers like myself would shoot as many coots and water hens as we could on the chalk streams merely because they had the habit of suddenly bursting out across the water right from under the angler's feet just as he was about to make the telling cast to a feeding fish. Not that trout are unused to these jittery birds, but the sudden dash across the water signals danger to the riverside community.

Any moving shadow means danger to the trout, be it from rod, line or angler. In places where trout are used to humans, they will often merely sink a little lower and remain seemingly indifferent to their presence. Indeed, George and his fishy friends who live below the bridge near my home are uncatchable for most of the time when approached from the river bank, but if a cast is made from the bridge one, or perhaps two, will fall for the trick before the message gets around.

It is quite funny to watch these wary fish at the start of the season. The bridge is crossed over by thousands of people who stop to eat their lunch. Bits of sandwiches are thrown in the water and walking sticks are waved. On the first day of the season, fish will be caught from the banks below the bridge, but come the next day and any sign of a waving rod or stick will send the trout scurrying for cover. It takes weeks before perhaps just the odd one will be caught. Who says trout have no memory?

Not only does the rod and line move-

Right: Casting a dry fly from directly behind the fish.

ment cause problems but so too does the shattering of the mirror effect when fly, leader and line all land on the water – and that is why the traditional upstream cast made in English dry fly fishing came on the scene.

The more directly below your fish, and the more accurately you cast, the better the chances of getting your fly to the fish unseen. The only problem then being its final arrival in the fish's window. Any attempts to cast to one side with a curve in the leader will make the mirror distort, spooking the trout, and this is why we use the finest leaders we can when fishing the dry fly, since they keep surface distortion down to a minimum.

An approach from above, using the more modern slack line cast helps because the

Next page: A stealthy approach to a trout rising in a shallow ripple.

fly arrives first followed by the leader.

Realising just how sharp a trout's senses are should make us ask ourselves these questions. Are there any bushes to hide behind, are we going to cast a shadow, are there any water birds between us and the fish, will the fly make a wake on the surface and is there a place to land the fish?

Individual lies with special peculiarities will also demand other measures, but follow these five basic rules and your chances of catching the fish are increased enormously.

Just because you own a pair of waders does not mean you automatically have to plunge into the water. It is a fact of modern fly fishing life that an awful lot of fish are scared away before the angler gets within casting range apart from the damage the angler's boots are doing to the delicate ecology of the stream. So only wade if you really have to. We have no such problems on my water as it is banned, and has been for centuries.

I well remember one angler I christened The Hippo, who fished on another water I looked after. When chest waders came on the scene, Hippo had to have a pair. We had just the one pool where wading was permitted and every time Hippo fished he would walk in at the pool's head and wade right down to the bottom stirring up mud, fish and everything else before doing the same in reverse order.

Funny thing. Hippo could never work out why he could not catch a trout, despite my advice to go to the bottom of the pool before plunging in. How different was his clumsy and unthinking approach to that of another angler I watched on a very difficult stretch of the Lathkill. This part of the river has built-up banks, sparse bank-side vegetation and the most crystal clear water you can imagine, so to get within range is an art in itself.

What this clever angler did was quite simple, he crept along the bank keeping low until he reached a spot where more than one fish was busy feeding. Then he just sat down and waited until the trout, alarmed at even his cautious approach, started to feed again. Using a low side-cast to keep shadows and flash right down, he would cast his fly to each feeding fish in turn and in the space of two hours took half a dozen quality trout without moving so much as an inch.

This particular stretch of water is quite slow-moving and the fish tend to cruise more than they normally would in swifter flow, but the technique can be used any-where that demands a careful approach.

So really, the way to get close enough to a feeding fish is to follow the old fashioned kerb drill of stop, look and listen, then if all is clear, proceed. A little more of this and a little less of rushing up and down the bank and the success rate of more than one fly fisher would soar.

Opposite: Wading carefully on the River Nidd in Yorkshire.

Setting the hook

While the odd fish will hook itself, we have to pull the hook home ourselves with a definite pull. For this to be instantaneous, the fly line must be under total control from the moment it lands on the water.

As the line slows down just before it lands on the water, it is a good idea to grip the line and to transfer it so that it runs over the index or second finger of the rod hand. Now, as the recovered line slides over the sensitive fingers, the tiniest pluck or tap will be registered instantly and the rod lifted smartly to set the hook.

This is not really the ideal method of bite indication. Watching the fly itself or the line is a far better plan rather than relying on the pull of an interested trout. Indeed, I believe that any fish hooked by touch has hooked itself, but be that as it may, when the strike has to made, the line is always under complete control if you use the touch method, taking just a moment to trap the line with the fingers on the rod hand. A word of caution, do not trap the line against the rod handle too hard as the strike is made or there is every chance of breaking the leader. With this danger in mind, I much prefer to carry the line over the second finger so that it is squeezed between a pair of fingers as you lift. This does not lock the line quite so tightly, but allows a running fish to take line, even if it does burn your fingers at times.

Strike really is not the word to use when setting the hook, as it implies a wild slash

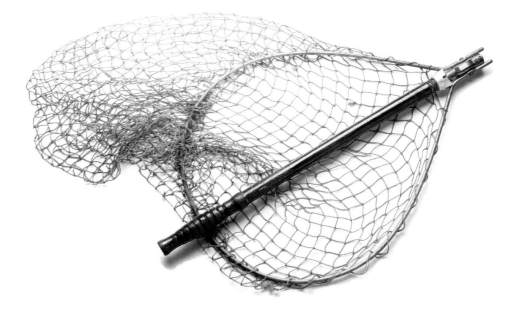

Right: A stream fisher's flick-up net.

with the rod, rather than the desired firm and controlled lift of the rod coupled with the line being drawn backwards with the other hand. An experienced angler completes this marriage of movements with a minimum of fuss, putting him in total control of his tackle at all times.

Once the strike is made, the fish will dictate the next move. If it races off, let it go under the greatest pressure you dare with the fingers holding the line until all the spare line has been run out and the fish is taking fly line from the reel. Pressure can then be applied by palming the reel spool rim until the fish tires. Then, the trout can be played off the reel, line being gradually recovered. With a big fish, it is sometimes necessary to "pump" the fish to recover any line at all. This is done by carefully lifting the rod after it has first been lowered to the horizontal. As soon as some line is gained and wound onto the reel, the rod tip is lowered again for another lift. Always be ready for the heavy trout that suddenly decides it does not like this sort of treatment and bolts when the rod is low, a sure recipe for disaster unless you give slack line.

Right: A Tasmanian Brown Trout.

Catch and release

This is a fairly modern idea based on the premise that any fish is far too valuable to be caught just the once, a phrase coined by catch and release advocate Lee Wulff.

While I realise that it is necessary to conserve natural stocks and frequently put fish back myself, I firmly believe that it is wrong to fish at all unless you intend taking it home to eat. If you wish to restrict your bag, then better to restrict the methods you use rather than to keep hooking and releasing fish all day as part of a numbers game.

The water I manage is a dry fly only fishery and this rule itself does restrict the number of fish caught, although there are times when the fish do take freely and then I think it more sporting to select the trout you want to catch rather than to fish at random. Surely, where is the skill or reason in fooling a lot of immature trout feeding in a frenzy on a big hatch of flies just to put them back?

Many English fisheries impose a bag limit that demands all fish caught being killed and kept with nothing being returned. When practised on a small, regularly stocked water it is a good idea as the fish are not as strong as wild fish and will die even if they are returned carefully.

To a degree, these sort of fisheries are merely an exercise in selling fish and should be recognised as being just that. In larger waters and rivers where the fish are fitter, trout can be confidently returned provided of course they are not handled or bleeding.

Like all wild things, trout live with danger, and to be hooked and played with care does little or no lasting damage, provided of course that they are returned without being taken from the water. It is not uncommon to find trout that have been severely damaged by herons behaving quite normally and feeding as if nothing had happened to them.

To eat is to live and there is little room for sentiment in the animal kingdom, but neither is there greed, something that we humans have a great capacity for. Take only what you need and leave no sign that you have been there and Nature will accept you. Do the opposite and eventually She will repay you for your folly.

Opposite: Carefully returning a trout to fight another day.

Next page: Perfection in every way.

CATCHING THE BEST FISH

With surface feeding fish, it is not all that difficult to spot the biggest fish but size can also be judged quite accurately by watching how much water is displaced by the fish as it turns.

Even when sipping in small flies off the surface, a larger fish will move a lot more water than a smaller one, making the water roll around the actual rise itself. Not something easy to describe, but once seen, will serve you well when looking for a better fish. Much the same goes for a fish feeding sub-surface. As I say, there is a lot more to successful fly fishing than casting a line and choosing the right fly.

Right: Landing nets should only be used if the trout is to be kept.

LANDING YOUR PRIZE

The landing net should be in the water ready to receive the beaten trout – but only if you intend taking the fish. As it starts to turn on its side, draw the trout over the net and lift it slowly until the fish is enveloped in the net but not yet quite clear of the water. Pull the net towards you and slide it up onto the bank away from the water's edge. Put down your rod and net, take your priest and kill the fish with a single sharp blow on the top of its head just behind the eyes.

Do this before you remove the hook from a dead fish as it is much easier to remove a hook from a still fish than a lively one, and more importantly, it is a matter of showing respect for a beautiful creature.

You may well be going to kill it for food, but there is no need whatever to let it suffer unnecessary stress once out of its environment which is what of course happens with commercially netted fish.

If you do not want to kill the trout, then it should never be taken from the water. Any fish to be returned should be played as quickly as possible so as not to tire it completely. As soon as it can be drawn to the bank, grasp the leader and slide your

Left: A superb trout from an Irish lough.

hand down until the hook is reached. Grip the hook and slip it out of the trout's jaw, preferably without touching the fish at all.

If the fish is large, it is often possible to grip the front of the trout's jaw and then to lay down the rod and to remove the hook with the free hand before steering the fish into the current. Any fish bleeding from the gills or the root of the tongue should be killed, as it will almost certainly die.

PREPARING YOUR CATCH

Trout is a gourmet's delight if it is properly prepared before cooking and a disaster if it is not. When you catch your fish, kill it quickly and clean it thoroughly, being sure to remove the gills as well as the innards but leave the head on.

Do this by pushing the point of a sharp knife into the vent and slice through the belly skin all the way to where the gill plates meet under the throat.

Ease everything out, cutting the system at the throat and then run the point around the join between the body and the gills leaving intact a half-moon shaped bone. Remove the gills and finally, run the knife down the dark line found along the backbone. This is the trout's kidney and will ruin the taste of the fish if it is left in.

MY FAVOURITE RECIPE

In my house, we like to eat our trout poached – how appropriate for a keeper on a trout stream!

This recipe, serving three people, needs three portion sized trout, a small onion, half a pint of dry cider, a bay leaf, a lemon, 2oz of butter and some parsley for a garnish.

Clean and wipe the trout leaving the head intact. Lay the fish in an oven-proof dish and scatter over the sliced onion. Add the cider, bay leaf and two or three lemon slices. Dot the top with butter and cover with either a lid or foil before baking in a moderate oven (Mark 4 or 350°F) for about 35 minutes.

Remove the bay leaf and the lemon and serve after adding more fresh lemon and the sprinkle of parsley. This simple dish is delicious eaten hot either with new season potatoes and fresh young broad beans or allowed to cool and served with a salad.

Left: Fishing in Ireland, where everything stops for tea.

Index

Acknowledgments

Some of the flies described in this book originated in excess of a hundred years ago. They have withstood the test of time, technology, and "anglers myth" to remain as effective today as they have ever been.

For authenticity, the fly tying materials used are to the original and traditional recipes. These naturally occurring materials were originally chosen for their known behaviour and colouration when immersed in the water, and proven effectiveness over many years of subsequent use.

In certain countries, alternative or synthetic materials may be substituted if the original materials are not available, or are protected by law.

PHOTOGRAPHY

Chris Allen: Covers, End Papers,
Pages - 1, 2, 3, 5 (BC), 20, 23 (C), 24, 25 (C), 28, 30, 52 and 78.
Russel Symons: Pages - 4, 19, 22, 23 (BL & TR), 90-91 and 92-93.
Peter Gathercole: Pages - 12-13, 27, 48, 49, 58, 61, 65, 77, 85, 88-89 and 94.
Coloursport - Ed Baxter: Pages - 4-5 (T), 18, 25 (BR), 68 and 84.
Ardea London Limited - Pages - 9 (by Jean-Paul Ferrero), 11 and 36.
Optical Art - Simon Everett: Pages - 7, 15, 46 and 63.
Sporting Pictures (UK) Limited - Pages - 54 and 59 (by Simon Everett).
Arthur Oglesby: Page 82.   Kevin Cullimore: Page 73.
Still Moving Picture Company - SJ Whitehorne: Page 57.
Roy Shaw: Page 64.   Jon Beer: Page 21.
Jim Tyree: Pages - 51 and 69.   Advertising Archives - Page 10.

ILLUSTRATIONS

Linden Artists - Jane Pickering, Stuart Lafford.

Thank you to Mary White, Lathkill Tackle,
for supplying equipment and materials for photography.